T0400775

Weird Animal Diets

Blood-Eating Animals

by Teresa Klepinger

www.focusreaders.com

Focus Readers is distributed by North Star Editions:
sales@northstareditions.com | 888-417-0195

Produced for Focus Readers by Red Line Editorial.

Photographs ©: MerlinTuttle.org/Science Source, cover, 1; Shutterstock Images, 4, 7, 8, 13, 14, 17, 19, 20–21, 22, 25, 29; FLPA/Alamy, 11; Pally/Alamy, 27

Library of Congress Cataloging-in-Publication Data
Names: Klepinger, Teresa, author.
Title: Blood-eating animals / by Teresa Klepinger.
Description: Lake Elmo, MN : Focus Readers, [2022] | Series: Weird animal diets | Includes index. | Audience: Grades 2-3
Identifiers: LCCN 2021036598 (print) | LCCN 2021036599 (ebook) | ISBN 9781637390528 (hardcover) | ISBN 9781637391068 (paperback) | ISBN 9781637391600 (ebook) | ISBN 9781637392102 (pdf)
Subjects: LCSH: Bloodsucking animals--Juvenile literature.
Classification: LCC QL756.55 .K54 2022 (print) | LCC QL756.55 (ebook) | DDC 591.53--dc23
LC record available at https://lccn.loc.gov/2021036598
LC ebook record available at https://lccn.loc.gov/2021036599

Printed in the United States of America
Mankato, MN
012022

About the Author

Teresa Klepinger loves to learn about the amazing world we live in. Writing about it for kids makes it even more fun. She also enjoys helping kids write their own stories. She lives in Oregon with her family and a dog . . . and hopefully no blood-eating animals.

Table of Contents

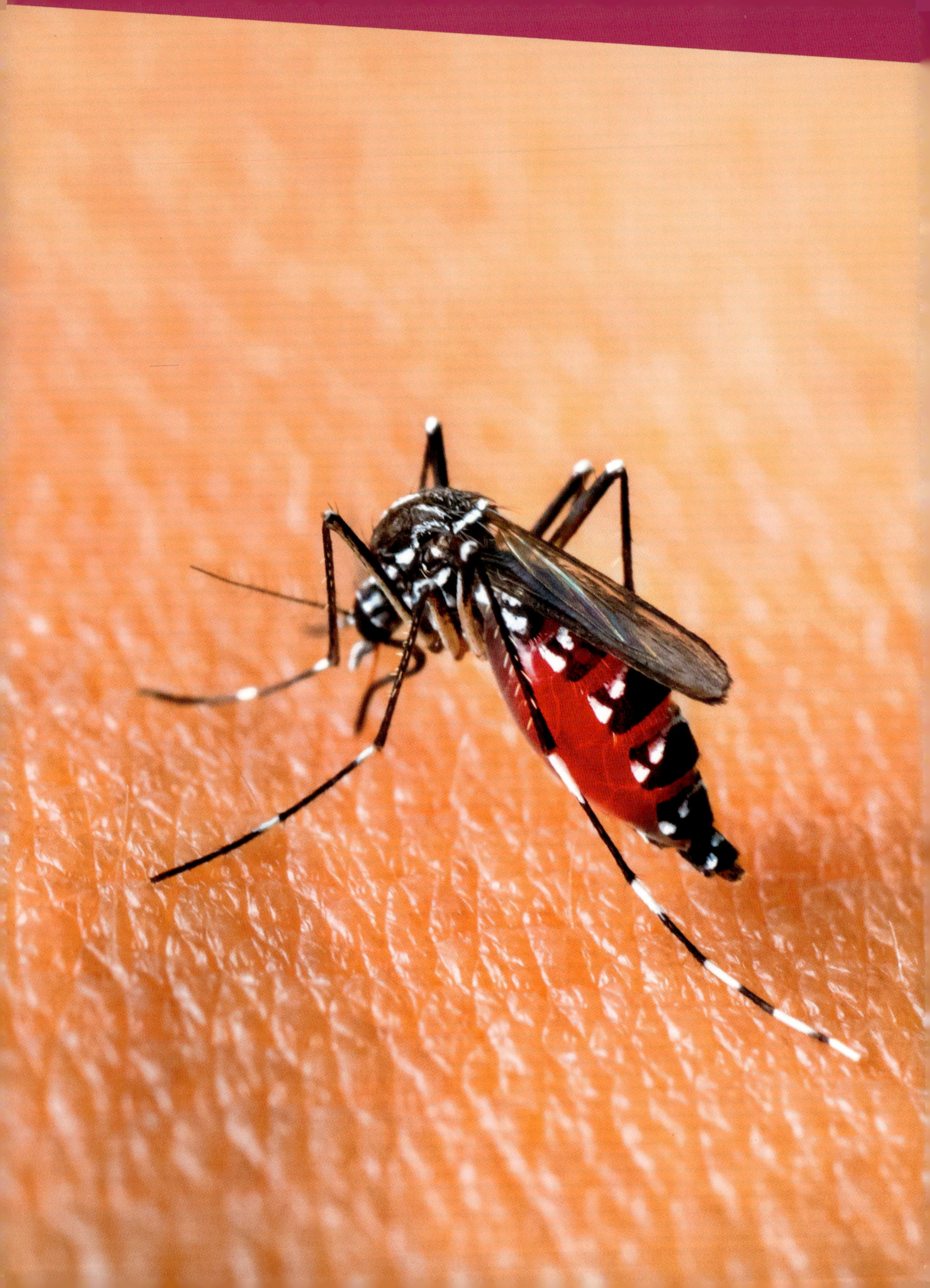

Chapter 1

A Tasty Meal

A mosquito lands on warm skin. She pokes it with her tube-shaped mouth. Then she begins sucking blood. Her bite leaves an itchy red bump. It might also leave behind a **disease**.

Mosquitoes often do sip feeding. They take a little blood from multiple people.

There are thousands of **species** of mosquitoes. Very few make people sick. But some mosquitoes' bites can spread **viruses**. The West Nile virus is one example. It can cause fever, head pains, and weakness.

Many animals eat blood. Some even eat human blood. They spread

Only female mosquitoes eat blood. They need it for laying eggs. Male mosquitoes drink plant nectar.

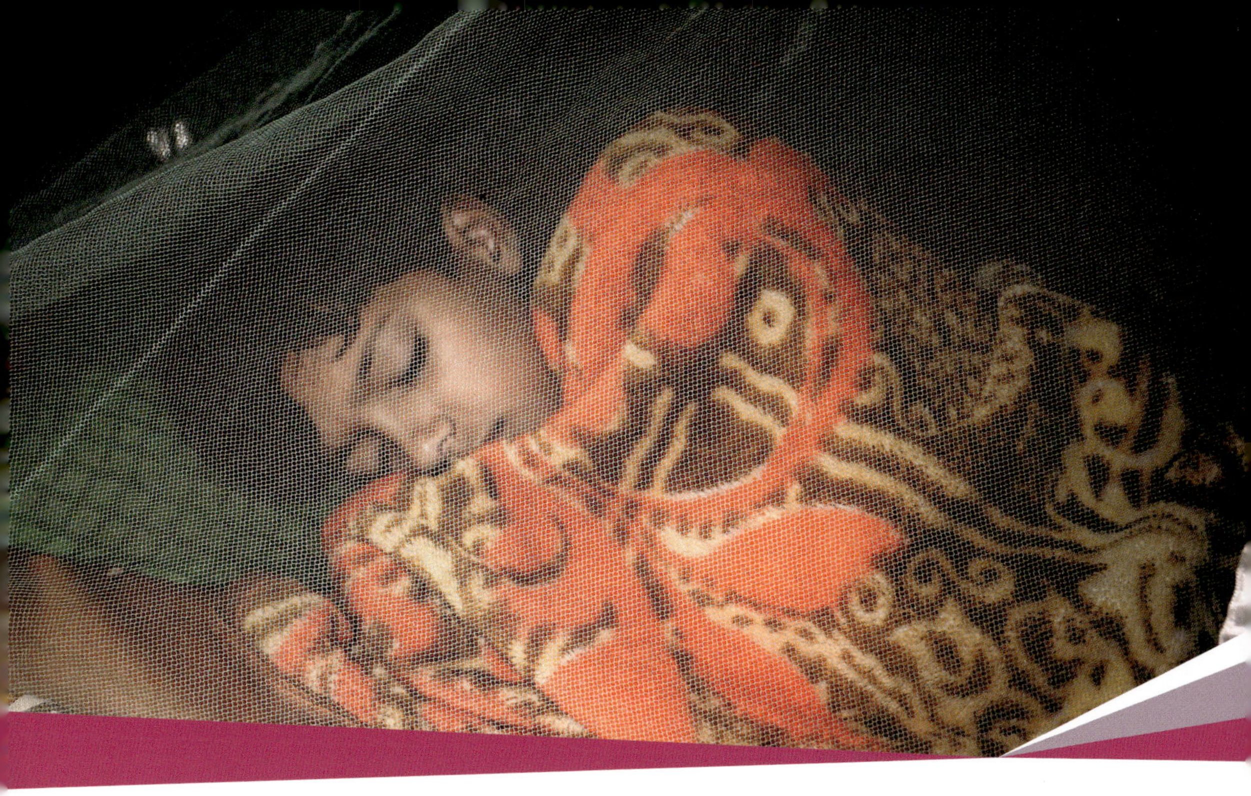

Some people sleep inside mosquito nets to stay safe from mosquitoes.

different diseases in this way. Scientists study blood-eating animals. They have learned ways to treat illnesses. They have even created new medicines. Their research has saved lives.

Chapter 2

Blood-Eaters That Fly

Many flying animals eat blood. For example, vampire bats are the only **mammals** that eat nothing but blood. They feed mostly on sleeping animals. Sometimes they feed on humans.

Vampire bats live in Mexico, Central America, and South America. They can sense the heat of blood.

First, a vampire bat chooses its meal. The bat's sharp teeth cut the animal's skin. The cut is tiny. The animal hardly feels it. Then, the bat laps up the blood. The bat's **saliva** has a **protein** called draculin. It keeps the blood from **clotting**. That way, the bat can drink until it is full.

Did You Know?

Scientists are studying draculin. They hope to make drugs from it. The drugs could help people with diseases.

Vampire moths are found mostly in Asia, eastern Africa, and parts of Europe.

Vampire moths suck juice out of fruit. But the males also suck blood. The male pierces an animal's skin.

Then he rocks back and forth to saw deeper. He drinks blood for up to 50 minutes.

Vampire moths sometimes drink human blood. But these bites are not harmful. A person just gets a sore spot after a bite.

Oxpeckers are African birds. They ride on big animals such as rhinos, zebras, and giraffes. They eat dead skin and earwax. They also eat bugs off the animals. In this way, oxpeckers rid the animals of **pests**.

Three oxpeckers pick bugs off an African buffalo.

But they also peck at sores on their **hosts**. Oxpeckers drink blood from the sores. Sometimes they even create new sores.

Chapter 3

Blood-Eaters That Crawl

Some blood-eating animals crawl. For instance, fleas live around the world. There are more than 2,500 species of fleas. All of them eat blood. Fleas jump onto people and animals. They bite their hosts.

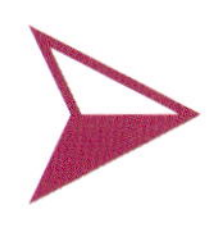

The cat flea is the most common flea in the United States. Adult fleas can jump the length of a piece of paper.

Then they drink their hosts' blood. These bites can be very itchy. They make people and animals scratch. Some flea species pass diseases to people. The diseases spread through a bite or the flea's poop.

Kissing bugs drink blood, too. They live in the southern United States. They are also in Mexico, Central America, and South America. The bugs often bite people's faces. This is why they are called kissing bugs.

Kissing bugs can spread Chagas disease. This disease can be mild or long-lasting.

Kissing bugs can spread disease. The bugs might poop after they eat. People might rub the itchy bites.

They could spread poop into their eyes, noses, or mouths. This could make them sick.

Bedbugs hide where people sleep. At night, they come out to bite and drink blood. Bedbugs mostly feed on humans. But they also feed on other animals. Their

Some people try to **starve** bedbugs. They stay away from their beds. But bedbugs can wait for months to eat. This makes them hard to get rid of.

Bedbugs tend to live in bed frames and other places close to where people sleep.

bites are painless. But some people get itchy spots from the bites. Luckily, bedbugs do not give people diseases.

ANIMAL SPOTLIGHT

Blood-Eating Jumping Spider

One jumping spider in East Africa eats human blood. But it doesn't bite humans. It doesn't even have the mouth parts to do so. Instead, it hunts mosquitoes that have sucked human blood. The spider eats the species of mosquitoes that give people malaria. Malaria is a disease. It makes people sick with fever, chills, and pains.

The spider recognizes these mosquitoes by sight. It hunts only the females that have blood in them. But sometimes, the spider can't find mosquitoes. Then, it drinks nectar from plants.

There are thousands of species of jumping spiders.

Chapter 4

Blood-Eaters That Swim

Some blood-eating animals swim. A sea lamprey has rings of teeth in its mouth. The teeth hook onto a fish's side. The lamprey scrapes away skin with its tongue. Then it drinks the fish's blood.

Sea lampreys used to live only in the Atlantic Ocean. Now they are also in the Great Lakes of North America.

Lampreys' saliva is similar to vampire bats' saliva. It keeps the blood flowing as they drink. Lampreys often kill the fish they feed on. But some lamprey species do not kill the fish.

A leech is a kind of worm. It lives mostly in fresh water. Leeches stick

One type of leech has a strong protein in its saliva. The protein thins blood. Scientists copied the protein. They use it to help sick people.

A leech sucks blood from a human hand.

to the skin of an animal. Then they bite to drink the animal's blood. These bites are painless. Leeches numb the skin. So, the animal can't feel a thing.

Doctors have used leeches throughout history. Today, doctors sometimes put leeches on wounds. The leeches drink the stale blood. This lets fresh blood come to the area. It helps the wound heal.

The tongue-eating louse lives in the ocean. The creature swims inside a fish's gills. These are the openings that a fish uses to breathe. Then the louse sticks to the fish's tongue. It sucks blood from the tongue. Finally, the tongue

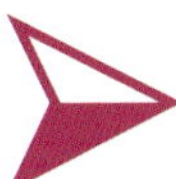

A tongue-eating louse has replaced the tongue of this Clark's anemonefish.

falls off. The louse stays inside the fish's mouth. It acts as the fish's tongue. The fish can live this way for the rest of its life.

FOCUS ON

Blood-Eating Animals

Write your answers on a separate piece of paper.

1. Write a letter to a friend explaining how doctors have used leeches to help people.
2. Which blood-eating animal do you find the most interesting? Why?
3. How does the tongue-eating louse enter a fish?
   - **A.** through its mouth
   - **B.** through its gills
   - **C.** through its skin
4. Why might a leech numb the skin of the animal it is biting?
   - **A.** The animal will be less likely to notice the leech and harm it.
   - **B.** The animal will be more likely to notice the leech and harm it.
   - **C.** The animal will bleed more quickly.

5. What does **medicines** mean in this book?

*They have learned ways to treat illness. They have even created new **medicines**.*

A. classes people take to learn something new

B. viruses that cause disease

C. drugs people can take to feel better

6. What does **pierces** mean in this book?

*The male **pierces** an animal's skin. Then he rocks back and forth to saw deeper.*

A. cuts into or through something

B. moves back and forth

C. sees far away

Answer key on page 32.

Glossary

clotting
Sticking together to form a thick mass.

disease
An illness or sickness.

hosts
Animals that other animals live on or in.

mammals
Animals that have hair and produce milk for their young.

pests
Unwanted insects or other animals that cause harm.

protein
A substance in the body that tells a living cell what to do.

saliva
The spit in an animal's mouth, often used for chewing and swallowing.

species
Groups of animals or plants of the same kind.

starve
To cause a living thing to suffer or die from hunger.

viruses
Tiny substances that can cause illness in people and animals.

To Learn More

BOOKS

Duhig, Holly. *Blood and Guts.* Minneapolis: Lerner Publications, 2020.

Mattern, Joanne. *Animal Appetites*. South Egremont, MA: Red Chair Press, 2020.

Stewart, Melissa. *Ick! Delightfully Disgusting Animal Dinners, Dwellings, and Defenses*. Washington, DC: National Geographic Kids, 2020.

NOTE TO EDUCATORS

Visit **www.focusreaders.com** to find lesson plans, activities, links, and other resources related to this title.

Index

Answer Key: 1. Answers will vary; **2.** Answers will vary; **3.** B; **4.** A; **5.** C; **6.** A